Mathematics Olympiad

Highly useful for all school students participating
in Various Olympiads & Competitions

Series Editor Keshav Mohan
Author Vibhu Singhal

Class
1

arihant

ARIHANT PRAKASHAN, MEERUT

ARIHANT PRAKASHAN, MEERUT
All Rights Reserved

卐 Administrative & Production Offices

Regd. Office   'Ramchhaya' 4577/15, Agarwal Road, Darya Ganj New Delhi -110002
Tele: 011- 47630600, 43518550; Fax: 011- 23280316

Head Office   Kalindi, TP Nagar, Meerut (UP) - 250002
Tele: 0121-2401479, 2512970, 4004199; Fax: 0121-2401648

All disputes subject to Meerut (UP) jurisdiction only.

卐 Sales & Support Offices

Agra, Ahmedabad, Bengaluru, Bhubaneswar, Bareilly, Chennai, Delhi, Guwahati, Haldwani, Hyderabad, Jaipur, Jhansi, Kolkata, Kota, Lucknow, Meerut, Nagpur & Pune

卐 ISBN   978-93-5094-409-7

卐 Price   ₹50.00

Typeset by Arihant DTP Unit at Meerut
Printed & Bound by Arihant Publications (I) Ltd. (Press Unit)

Production Team

Publishing Manager	Amit Verma	Page Layouting	Mudit Rastogi
Project Coordinator	Shelly Singhal	Figure Illustrator	Brahampal Singh
Cover Designer	Syed Darin Zaidi	Proof Reader	Rachi Aggarwal
Inner Designer	Ravi Negi		

For further information about Arihant Books
log on to www.arihantbooks.com or email to info@arihantbooks.com

Preface

Mathematics Olympiad Series for Class 1st-10th is a series of books which will challenge the young inquisitive minds by the non-routine and exciting mathematical problems.

The main purpose of this series is to make the students ready for competitive exams. The school/board exams are of qualifying nature but not competitive, they do not help the students to prepare for competitive exams, which mainly have objective questions.

- **Need of Olympiad Series**
  This series will fill this gap between the school/board and competitive exams as this series have all questions in Objective format. This series helps students who are willing to sharpen their problem solving skills. Unlike typical assessment books, which emphasis on drilling practice, the focus of this series is on practicing problem solving techniques.

- **Development of Logical Approach**
  The thought provoking questions given in this series will help students to attain a deeper understanding of the concepts and through which students will be able to impart Reasoning/Logical/Analytical skills in them.

- **Complement Your School Studies**
  This series complements the additional preparation needs of students for regular school/board exams. Along with, it will also address all the requirements of the students who are approaching National/State level Olympiads.

I shall welcome criticism from the students, teachers, educators and parents. I shall also like to hear from all of you about errors and deficiencies, which may have remained in this edition and the suggestions for the next edition.

Editor

Contents

1. Play with Numbers 1-7

2. Addition 8-14

3. Subtraction 15-21

4. Length 22-25

5. Weight 26-29

6. Time and Calendar 30-35

7. Money 36-41

8. Shapes and Patterns 42-47

9. Picture Graphs 48-51

Practice Sets (1-2) 52-59

Answers 60

1

Play with Numbers

1. Count the fruits and mark the correct number.

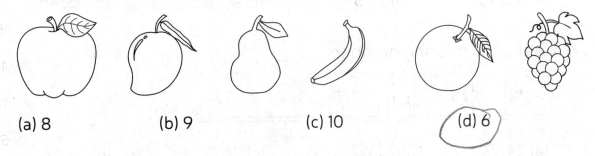

   (a) 8   (b) 9   (c) 10   (d) 6

2. Which of the following words contain  letters?

   (a) SHAPES   (b) CALENDAR   (c) MONEY   (d) CIRCLES

3. Which of the following boxes contain 4 things?

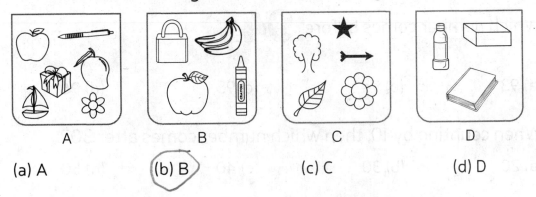

     A   B   C   D

   (a) A   (b) B   (c) C   (d) D

4. Find the missing number in the given figure.

    (a) 32   (b) 36   (c) 39   (d) 40

5. Select the missing numbers from the given options.

    (a) 42, 45   (b) 51, 54   (c) 40, 43   (d) 45, 48

6. Write the missing numbers.

72		73	74		75		76		77

    (a) 74, 76   (b) 73, 77   (c) 76, 75   (d) 73, 78

7. What number comes in between in the given figure?

    (a) 82   (b) 84   (c) 85   (d) 86

8. Which number comes before ?

    (a) 93   (b) 94   (c) 95   (d) 96

9. When counting by 10, then which number comes after 30?

    (a) 20   (b) 30   (c) 40   (d) 50

10. When counting by 2, then which number comes just before 20 ?

(a) 16   (b) 18   (c) 22   (d) 24

11. What number comes just before ⟨ 70 ⟩ ?

(a) 69   (b) 71   (c) 72   (d) 68

A   B   C   D   E

12. 14   25   9   36   19

Which block has the highest number on it?

(a) B   (b) C   (c) D   (d) E

13. Which balloon has smallest number on it?

20   19   32   4

(a)   (b)   (c)   (d)

14. Arrange the following numbers in ascending order and select the correct option.

32   10   49   51   17

(a) 49 51 32 10 17   (b) 51 49 32 17 10

(c) 10 17 32 49 51   (d) 51 49 17 32 10

15. How many tens are there in 43?

(a) 4   (b) 3   (c) 7   (d) 0

16. Arrange the given pages of a book in their correct order.

(a) | 18 | 32 | 29 | 40 | 51 |

(b) | 18 | 29 | 32 | 40 | 51 |

(c) | 18 | 40 | 32 | 29 | 51 |

(d) | 18 | 40 | 51 | 32 | 29 |

17. Arrange the given numbers in descending order and choose the correct option.

| 36 | 12 | 24 | 42 | 19 |

(a) | 12 | 19 | 24 | 36 | 42 |

(b) | 42 | 36 | 12 | 24 | 19 |

(c) | 12 | 24 | 19 | 36 | 42 |

(d) | 42 | 36 | 24 | 19 | 12 |

18. [?] tens + [9] ones = [59]

(a) 4   (b) 5   (c) 6   (d) 14

19. Tom saw a traffic signboard with a number written on it.

SPEED
LIMIT
78

What is the place value of 8 in the number 78?

(a) Ones   (b) Tens   (c) Hundred   (d) Zero

20. The place value of 2 in 72 is _____ .

(a) tens   (b) ones   (c) zero   (d) seventh

21. 64 is same as _____ .

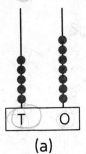 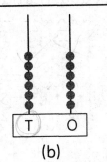 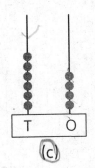 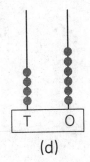

(a)　　　　　(b)　　　　　(c)　　　　　(d)

22. Which abacus shows 1 more than 20?

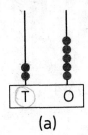 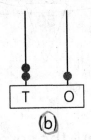 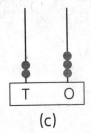 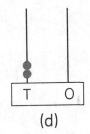

(a)　　　　　(b)　　　　　(c)　　　　　(d)

23. Which abacus shows 1 less than 20?

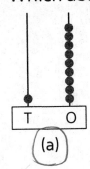 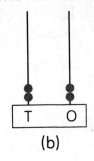 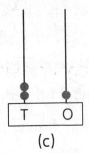 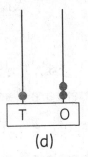

(a)　　　　　(b)　　　　　(c)　　　　　(d)

24. Which two baskets have equal number of objects kept in them?

(a)

(c)

(b)

(d)

25. Which two figures given below have equal numbers of dots?

(a)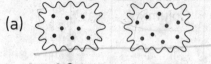

(b)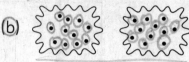

(c)

(d)

26. I am greater than 45 but less than 50. What number am I?

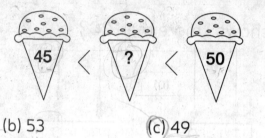

(a) 40   (b) 53   (c) 49   (d) 44

27. Study the figures given below and mark the correct answer.

  (a) There are 4 flower pots and 3 apples

  (b) There are 4 apples and 4 flower pots

  (c) There are 4 apples and 3 flower pots

  (d) There are 3 apples and 3 flower pots

28. Study the figure given below and mark the correct answer.

  (a) Number of △ is equal to number of ○

  (b) Number of △ is less than number of ○

  (c) Number of ○ is less than number of △

  (d) Number of △ is more than number of ○

29. Match the equal number of objects given in column I and column II.

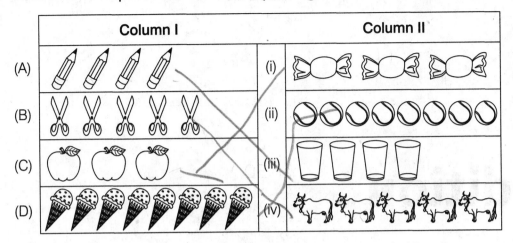

	(A)	(B)	(C)	(D)
(a)	(iv)	(iii)	(ii)	(i)
(b)	(iii)	(iv)	(i)	(ii)
(c)	(i)	(ii)	(iii)	(iv)
(d)	(ii)	(iv)	(iii)	(i)

30. Match the number of objects given in column I with numbers given in column II.

Column I	Column II

	Column I		Column II
(A)	🥣🥣🥣	(i)	4
(B)	▭▭▭▭	(ii)	2
(C)	⚪⚪	(iii)	3
(D)	☆☆☆☆☆☆	(iv)	8
(E)	🌙🌙🌙🌙🌙🌙🌙🌙	(v)	6

	(A)	(B)	(C)	(D)	(E)
(a)	(i)	(ii)	(iii)	(iv)	(v)
(b)	(ii)	(v)	(iv)	(iii)	(i)
(c)	(iii)	(i)	(ii)	(v)	(iv)
(d)	(iii)	(i)	(ii)	(iv)	(v)

2
Addition

1. Which number should be written in place of ❓ ?

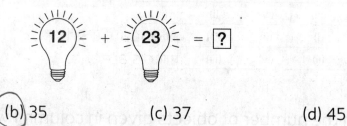

$$12 + 23 = \boxed{?}$$

(a) 36   (b) 35   (c) 37   (d) 45

2. Which of the following is the correct sum?

(a) $\boxed{6} + \boxed{2} = \boxed{8}$ (b) $\boxed{7} + \boxed{0} = \boxed{9}$

(c) $\boxed{5} + \boxed{3} = \boxed{7}$ (d) $\boxed{4} + \boxed{4} = \boxed{6}$

3. Count the balloons and mark the correct sum.

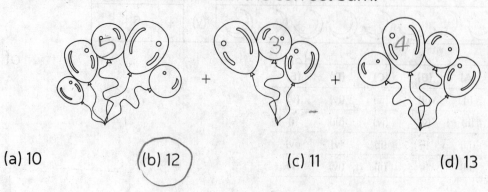

(a) 10   (b) 12   (c) 11   (d) 13

4. Total number of cups, plates and spoons are _____.

 + +

(a) 3 + 5 + 7   (b) 5 + 4 + 6   (c) 6 + 4 + 5   (d) 2 + 4 + 7

5. There are  blue balls and black balls in a box. How many total balls are there in a box?

(a) 7   (b) 8   (c) 9   (d) 10

6. Gauri bought 5 shirts on Monday, 4 shirts on Tuesday and 7 shirts on Wednesday. How many shirts are there with Gauri?

(a) 14   (b) 16   (c) 18   (d) 11

7. There are  mangoes in a basket. Rohan puts  more mangoes in it. How many mangoes are there in a basket now?

(a) 8   (b) 9   (c) 10   (d) 11

8. If  leaves are added to ⬥⬥⬥ , then total number of leaves are _____.

(a) 7   (b) 8   (c) 9   (d) 10

9. Reena has 5 ice-creams and Sunita has 3 ice-creams. How many ice-creams does they have together?

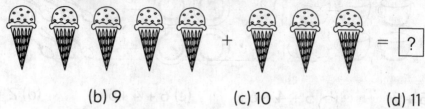

(a) 8   (b) 9   (c) 10   (d) 11

10. There are ⎡35⎤ students in class I A, ⎡32⎤ students in class I B. How many total students are there in class I?

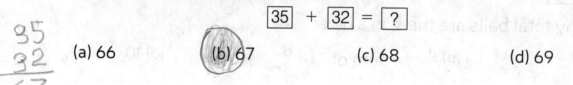

$$\boxed{35} + \boxed{32} = \boxed{?}$$

(a) 66   (b) 67   (c) 68   (d) 69

11. Study the pattern and fill the missing term ⎡?⎤ from the given options.

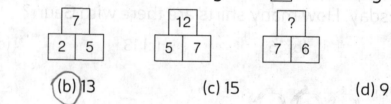

(a) 7   (b) 13   (c) 15   (d) 9

12. Add the numbers on the dice and mark their correct sum.

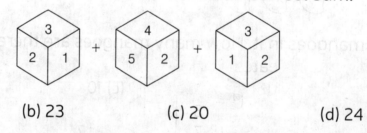

(a) 21   (b) 23   (c) 20   (d) 24

13. Choose the correct addition relation for the given figure.

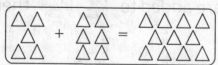

(a) 4 + 6 = 10   (b) 5 + 6 = 11   (c) 6 + 6 = 12   (d) 3 + 4 = 8

14. How many circles should be drawn in box B, so that the total circles in the boxes A and B becomes 15?

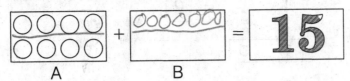

A   B

(a) ○ ○ ○ ○ ○ ○ ○

(b) ○ ○ ○ ○ ○

(c) ○ ○ ○ ○ ○ ○

(d) ○ ○ ○ ○

15. Which two cards give the sum of 12?

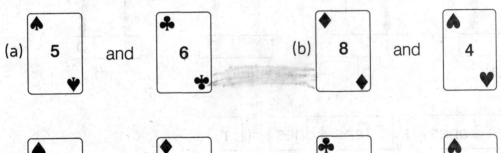

(a) ♠ 5 and ♣ 6   (b) ♦ 8 and ♥ 4

(c) ♥ 1 and ♦ 8   (d) ♣ 6 and ♥ 4

16. Which sum is greatest?

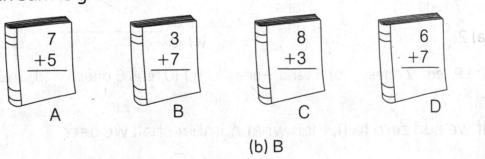

7	3	8	6
+5	+7	+3	+7
A	B	C	D

(a) A   (b) B

(c) C   (d) D

17. 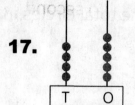 + 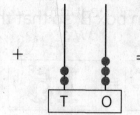 =

What is the value of ? ?

(a) 54   (b) 68   (c) 65   (d) 58

18. $\boxed{23 + 14}$ is shown by which abacus?

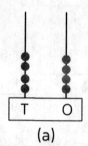 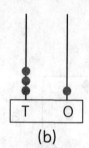 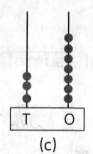 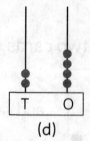

(a)   (b)   (c)   (d)

19. $\boxed{1 \text{ ten } 3 \text{ ones}}$ + $\boxed{2 \text{ tens } 3 \text{ ones}}$ = $\boxed{?}$

Which option will replace with ? ?

(a) 37   (b) 36   (c) 38   (d) 46

20. 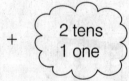 7 tens 8 ones + 2 tens 1 one equals to _____ .

(a) 9 tens 9 ones   (b) 8 tens 9 ones   (c) 10 tens 8 ones   (d) 7 tens 0 one

21. If we add zero to 11, then what number shall we get?

$$11 + 0 = \boxed{?}$$

(a) 0   (b) 11   (c) 10   (d) 9

22. Rohan jumps 4 steps in one move. Again, he jumps 5 steps in second move. On which number did Rohan reach now?

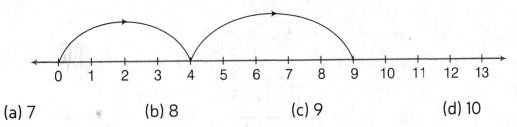

(a) 7   (b) 8   (c) 9   (d) 10

23. While playing Sumit takes 2 steps in one move. After the fourth move where will Sumit be?

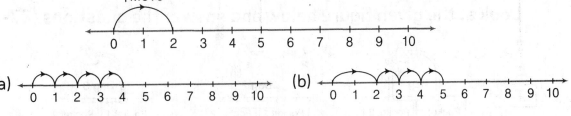

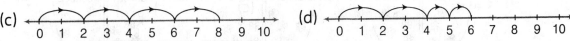

24. In which box " = " sign can be placed?

(a) 7 + 2 ☐ 4 + 5   (b) 3 + 9 ☐ 2 + 5

(c) 2 + 6 ☐ 3 + 4   (d) 7 + 1 ☐ 1 + 4

25. Arrange the given objects from greatest to smallest according to their sum.

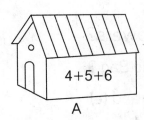

A

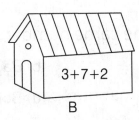

B

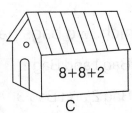

C

(a) A, B, C   (b) B, C, A

(c) C, A, B   (d) C, B, A

26. Look at the grid given below, where numbers are added across and down.

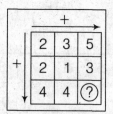

What number must be placed in ⍰ ?

(a) 7   (b) 6   (c) 8   (d) 9

Look at the given figure below and answer the questions (27-29).

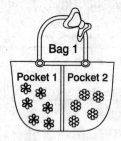 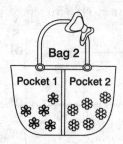 

27. How many flowers are there in Bag 2?

(a) 5   (b) 7   (c) 11   (d) 4

28. How many total flowers are there in all the bags?

(a) 32   (b) 30   (c) 34   (d) 38

29. Which two bags have the same number of flowers?

(a) Bag 1 and Bag 2   (b) Bag 1 and Bag 3

(c) Bag 2 and Bag 3   (d) Both (a) and (c)

3
Subtraction

1. Find the difference between the number of balls in each box.

 – 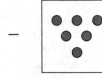 = ?

   (a) 3   (b) 4   (c) 5   (d) 6

2. Ali had **12** ducks out of which **4** died due to some disease.

How many ducks are left with Ali?

   (a) 7   (b) 8   (c) 9   (d) 10

3. Choose the correct number to fill in the place of ? .

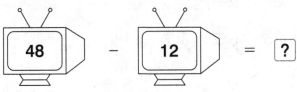

   (a) 37   (b) 36

   (c) 35   (d) 30

4.

How many fruits are left uncut?

(a) 4   (b) 5   (c) 6   (d) 7

5. Which of the following options will complete the number bond?

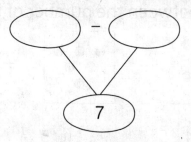

(a) 9, 3   (b) 6, 1   (c) 9, 2   (d) 8, 3

6. Choose the correct subtraction of leaves from the given options.

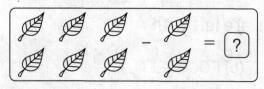

(a) 🍃 🍃 🍃 🍃

(b) 🍃 🍃 🍃 🍃 🍃

(c) 🍃 🍃

(d) 🍃 🍃 🍃 🍃 🍃 🍃 🍃 🍃

7. Which option given below is same as  ?

(a) 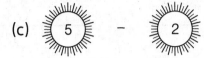   (b)

(c) 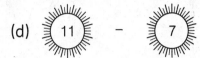   (d)

8. Select the correct subtraction from the options given below.

 –  =

(a) 15   (b) 10   (c) 11   (d) 16

9. What should be subtracted from 9 to make it 4?

(a) 5   (b) 6   (c) 7   (d) 8

10. The value of  SEVENTEEN – FOUR = ?

(a) THIRTEEN   (b) FOURTEEN   (c) FIFTEEN   (d) TWELVE

11. Which abacus shows 27 − 21 = 6?

(a) 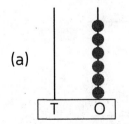   (b) 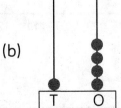   (c) 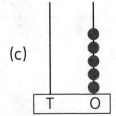   (d)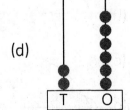

12. Which abacus shows $47 - 32 = 15$?

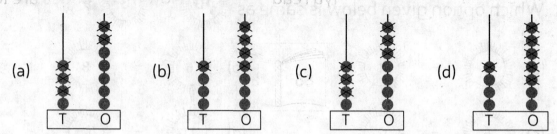

(a)　　　(b)　　　(c)　　　(d)

13. Ali jumps 9 steps forward. Again, he jumps 4 steps backward. On which number did Ali reach now?

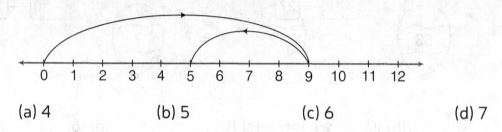

(a) 4　　　　(b) 5　　　　(c) 6　　　　(d) 7

14. 3 less than 10 is represented by which number line?

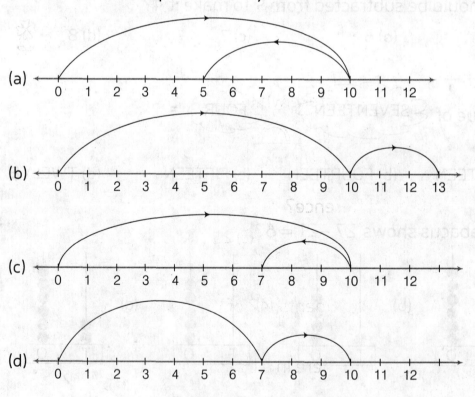

(a)

(b)

(c)

(d)

15. A book has 66 pages. Vinya read 35 pages. How many pages are left to read by Vinya?

(a) 20   (b) 32   (c) 31   (d) 34

16. Which of the following option is a correct match?

(a) 29 – 14 ⟶ 20   (b) 25 – 12 ⟶ 37   (c) 37 – 11 ⟶ 26   (d) 22 – 10 ⟶ 21

17. Salman had  flowers. He gave 🌸🌸 flowers

to his mother. How many are left with him?

(a) 🌸🌸🌸   (b) 🌸🌸🌸🌸

(c) 🌸🌸   (d) 🌸🌸🌸🌸🌸🌸🌸

18. Rachi has made some mistake while doing subtraction i.e.

79 – 54 = 28

What is the correct difference?

(a) 30   (b) 24   (c) 25   (d) 26

19. In a class, there are 84 students. 42 of them are .

How many are there in a class?

(a) 42   (b) 60   (c) 40   (d) 24

20. If 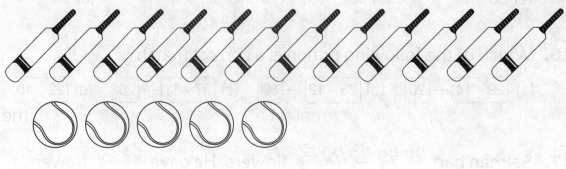 = 15 and | = 12, then which of the following shows △ – | ?

(a) 2   (b) 3   (c) 4   (d) 5

21. How many more balls are needed such that the number of bats and balls become equal?

(a) 7   (b) 5   (c) 12   (d) 17

22. There are   flower pots.

But   flower pots broke. How many flower pots are left?

(a) 10   (b) 7   (c) 3   (d) 4

23. How many softies should be crossed (✗) to show 4 softies uncrossed?

(a) 4   (b) 6   (c) 8   (d) 12

24. Ankit has 10 toffees. He eats 3 of them. Which of the following option shows the toffees left with Ankit?

(a) 10 + 3 = 13   (b) 10 + 3 = 12

(c) 10 – 3 = 7   (d) 10 – 3 = 8

25. 9 tens 3 ones − 6 tens 2 ones = ?

Choose the correct option for ?.

(a) 3 tens 1 one   (b) 4 tens 2 ones   (c) 1 one 3 tens   (d) 3 tens 7 ones

26.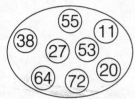

Difference between the greatest and the smallest numbers in the above collection is _____.

(a) 53   (b) 26   (c) 61   (d) 63

27. Number are subtracted across and down in the given grid.

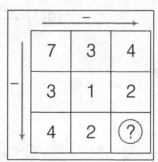

What number must be placed in ? ?

(a) 6   (b) 6   (c) 2   (d) 1

Length

1. Which is the longest key?

(a) 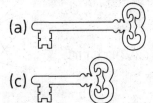　　　　　　(b)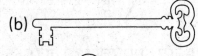

(c) 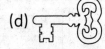　　　　　　(d)

2. Which is the tallest tree?

(a) 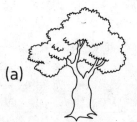　(b) 　(c) 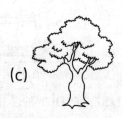　(d)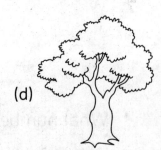

3. Which of the following cup is shortest?

(a) 　　(b) 　　(c) 　　(d)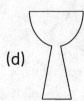

4. Which is the smallest triangle?

(a) 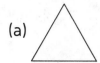　　(b) 　　(c) 　　(d) △

5. Which ice-cream is biggest?

(a) 　　(b) 　　(c) 　　(d)

6. Which kite has a shortest tail?

(a) 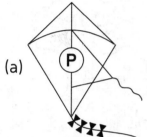　　(b) 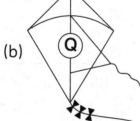　　(c) 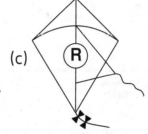　　(d)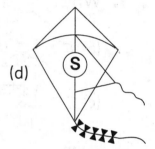

7. Which hammer is longer than hammer R?

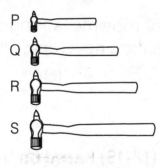

(a) P　　　　　(b) Q　　　　　(c) S　　　　　(d) Both P and Q

8. Length of the pencil is _____.

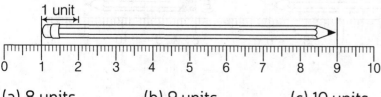

(a) 8 units　　　　(b) 9 units　　　　(c) 10 units　　　　(d) 7 units

9. The length of the ladder is _____ metres.

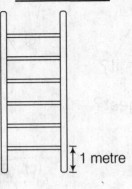

1 metre

(a) 6   (b) 7   (c) 8   (d) 9

10. Distance between tree A and tree B is _____ metre.

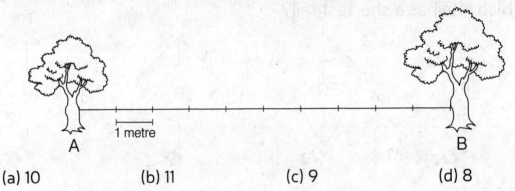

1 metre

A   B

(a) 10   (b) 11   (c) 9   (d) 8

11. Seema has two pieces of rope measuring 5 metres and 4 metres. She wants to join them to make a new rope. The length of new rope will be _____ metres.

(a) 10   (b) 9   (c) 6   (d) 7

Answer the questions (12-15) based on the given figure.

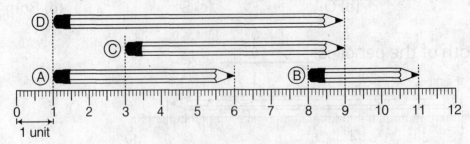

1 unit

12. Which is the longest pencil?

(a) A   (b) B   (c) C   (d) D

13. Which is the smallest pencil?

(a) A   (b) B   (c) C   (d) D

14. Pencil B is shorter than pencil C by _____ units.

(a) 2   (b) 3   (c) 4   (d) 5

15. The length of pencil D is _____ units.

(a) 7   (b) 8   (c) 9   (d) 10

16. Which butterfly is at the greatest distance from the wall?

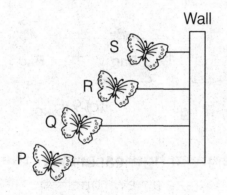

(a) P   (b) Q   (c) R   (d) S

17. Which candle is bigger than candle Q but shorter than candle P?

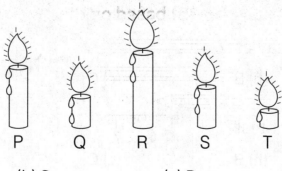

(a) T   (b) S   (c) R   (d) Both R and S

5
Weight

1. If the weight of a $\overset{\text{Bag}}{\Large\cap}$ = 4 kg. Then, the weighs of

(a) 8 kg   (b) 12 kg   (c) 15 kg   (d) 6 kg

On the basis of the given figures, answer the questions (2-4).

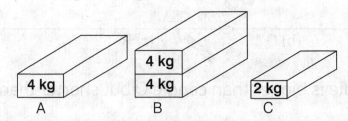

2. Which box is heaviest?

(a) A   (b) B   (c) C   (d) Can't tell

3. Which box is lightest?

(a) A   (b) B   (c) C   (d) Can't tell

4. Box B weighs _____ kg more than box C .

(a) 5   (b) 6   (c) 7   (d) 8

5. The heaviest among the following is _____ .

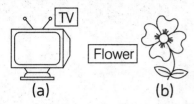 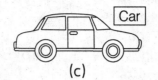 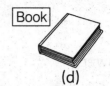

    (a)   (b)   (c)   (d)

6. Which of the following picture shows that ball 1 is lighter than ball 2?

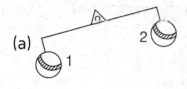 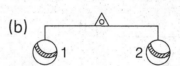

(a)   (b)

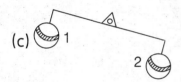

(c)   (d) None of these

7. Which of the following is heavier than the ball?

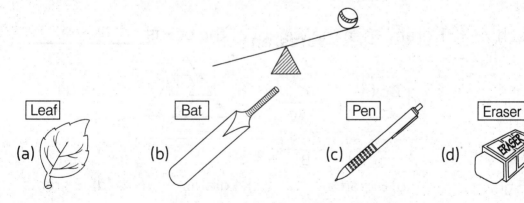

    (a)   (b)   (c)   (d)

8. 3 apples weighs as much as _____ mangoes.

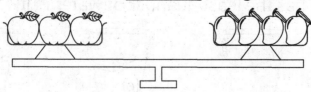

(a) 3   (b) 4   (c) 5   (d) 7

9. The heavier object is _____ .

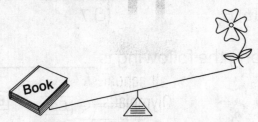

(a) Flower

(b) Book

(c) Both have same weight

(d) Can't tell

10. If weight of each 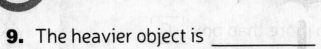 is equal to 1 unit, then the weight of book is _____ units.

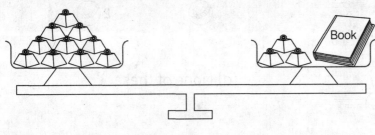

(a) 6   (b) 7   (c) 9   (d) 10

11. If each △ = 1 gram, then the weight of the box is _____.

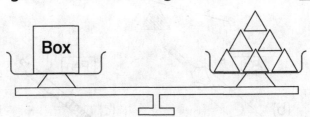

(a) 5 grams   (b) 6 grams   (c) 4 grams   (d) 12 grams

12. Which bucket has the least quantity of water in it?

(a)   (b)   (c)   (d)

13. Reena weighted 20 kg when she was 10 years old. After 5 years, she weighs 40 kg . The increase in weight of Reena is _____ .

(a) 10 kg   (b) 20 kg   (c) 30 kg   (d) 60 kg

Weight of the four baskets is shown below. On the basis of the weight of the baskets answer the questions (14-17).

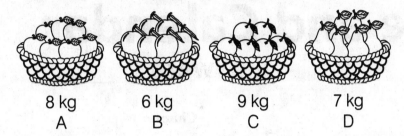

| 8 kg | 6 kg | 9 kg | 7 kg |
| A | B | C | D |

14. Which basket is heaviest?

(a) A   (b) B   (c) C   (d) D

15. Which basket is lightest?

(a) A   (b) B   (c) C   (d) D

16. Weight of basket A is _____ kg less than weight of basket C .

(a) 1   (b) 2   (c) 3   (d) 4

17. Weight of basket C is _____ kg more than weight of basket B .

(a) 1   (b) 2   (c) 3   (d) 4

6

Time and Calendar

1. Which day comes after Tuesday?

   (a) Monday   (b) Wednesday   (c) Thursday   (d) Friday

2. If yesterday was Sunday, then today is _____ .

   (a) Tuesday   (b) Monday   (c) Wednesday   (d) Friday

3. If yesterday was Friday, then tomorrow will be _____ .

   (a) Saturday   (b) Sunday   (c) Monday   (d) Thursday

4. How many days are there in a week?

   (a) 2 days   (b) 4 days   (c) 5 days   (d) 7 days

5. Which month comes just after sixth month of a year?

   (a) August   (b) July   (c) June   (d) December

6. _____ comes after July and before December.

   (a) November   (b) March   (c) January   (d) April

Use the following calendar to answer the questions (7-10).

SUN	MON	TUE	WED	THUR	FRI	SAT
	1	2	3	4	5	6
7	8	9	10	11	12	13
14	15	16	17	18	19	20
21	22	23	24	25	26	27
28	29	30	31			

7. How many Tuesdays are there in the given month?

(a) 4   (b) 5   (c) 6   (d) 7

8. If today is 9th of this month, then Rohan's birthday is on the 12th. How many days are left?

(a) 2   (b) 3   (c) 4   (d) 1

9. Third Saturday falls on which date of the given month?

(a) 6   (b) 13   (c) 20   (d) 27

10. The last day of the month is _____ .

(a) Tuesday   (b) Wednesday   (c) Thursday   (d) Saturday

11. A leap year has _____days.

(a) 365   (b) 366   (c) 28   (d) 31

12. Gopal's birthday is in February. On which of the following dates, his birthday cannot fall?

(a) 27 Feb   (b) 29 Feb   (c) 28 Feb   (d) 30 Feb

13. You go to sleep, when stars are shining in the sky. It must be _____ .

(a) day   (b) night   (c) morning   (d) afternoon

14. You do breakfast in the _____ .

(a) evening   (b) night   (c) morning   (d) afternoon

15. You go to school in the _____ .

(a) morning   (b) night   (c) evening   (d) afternoon

16. Which options shows correct sequences of doing following activities?

(a) Playing → Going to school → Bathing → Brushing

(b) Bathing → Brushing → Going to school → Sleeping

(c) Bathing → Going to school → Sleeping → Playing

(d) Brushing → Bathing → Breakfast → Going to school

17. Which activity is done at the right time?

(a) Breakfast at 2 O'clock in the night

(b) Sleeping at 6 O'clock in the evening

(c) Going to school at 7 O'clock in the morning

(d) Bathing at 5 O'clock in the evening

18. The Sun is just above your head. What time of the day is it?

(a) Morning

(b) Afternoon

(c) Evening

(d) Night

19. Study the following table to answer the given questions.

Boy	Chirag	Ishu	Shivam	Ankit
Time taken to reach the school	10 minutes	5 minutes	15 minutes	25 minutes

(i) Who will be third to reach school?

(a) Chirag

(b) Ishu

(c) Shivam

(d) Ankit

(ii) Who will take more time in going to school?

(a) Ankit

(b) Shivam

(c) Ishu

(d) Chirag

20. Which glass will take more time to be filled with milk?

(a)   (b)   (c)   (d)

21. When the short hand is at 4 and the long hand is at 12, the time is _____ .

(a) 3 O'clock

(b) 4 O'clock

(c) 5 O'clock

(d) 6 O'clock

22. The long hand takes _____ minutes to move from 2 to 3.

(a) 1   (b) 2   (c) 5   (d) 6

23. The long hand is pointing at _____minutes.

(a) 20

(b) 30

(c) 35

(d) 15

24. Which clock is showing 2 hours after 4 O'clock?

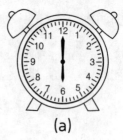   

(a)   (b)   (c)   (d)

25. Sheela started playing at 3 : 00 pm and finished playing at 4 : 30 pm. The time taken by her is _____ .

    (a) 1 hour 30 minutes   (b) 2 hours

    (c) 2 hours 30 minutes   (d) 30 minutes

26. After 12 hours, the hour hand will be on _____ .

    (a) 2   (b) 12   (c) 4   (d) 3

27. Ram started walking at 6 O'clock in the morning. He walks for one hour and then come back home. At what time, will he reach home?

    (a) 5 O' clock   (b) 6 O' clock

    (c) 7 O' clock   (d) 8 O' clock

28. Which time is called mid-night?

    (a) 11 O' clock in the night

    (b) 12 O' clock in the night

    (c) 12 O' clock in the day

    (d) 9 O' clock in the night

7

Money

1. The total money shown by the coins below is _____.

(a) ₹ 14   (b) ₹ 15   (c) ₹ 16   (d) ₹ 17

2.  ₹ 8 can be taken for _____.

(a)

(b)

(c)

(d)

3. Which toy has maximum cost?

₹ 50 (a)   ₹ 100 (b)   ₹ 35 (c)   ₹ 10 (d)

4. Which amount is less than ₹ 20?

(a)

(b)

(c)

(d)

5. Meena has with her. Her father gave

 to her. Total money Meena has now _____ .

(a)

(b) ₹ 20   ₹ 10   5   2

(c) ₹ 20   ₹ 20

(d) ₹ 10   ₹ 10   5   5

6. Sonal wants to exchange his ₹ 5 with some coins. Which set of coins can she take?

(a)

(b)

(c)

(d)

7. Ankit has ₹ 10 . He bought a pack of chips worth ₹ 5 . The money left with him is _____ .

(a) ₹ 4

(b) ₹ 5

(c) ₹ 2

(d) ₹ 6

8. Rohan gave ₹50 to buy the toy car. How much money will he get back?

(a) ₹ 15   (b) ₹ 20   (c) ₹ 10   (d) ₹ 40

9. One teddy bear costs ₹ 20. How many teddy bears can be bought for ₹ 40?

(a) 2   (b) 3   (c) 4   (d) 5

10. Cost of is ₹ 5. Then, cost of  is _____.

(a) ₹ 10   (b) ₹ 15   (c) ₹ 20   (d) ₹ 25

11. Purnima had ₹ 50. She bought 3 apples for ₹ 30. How much money is left with her?

(a) ₹ 20   (b) ₹ 30   (c) ₹ 40   (d) ₹ 10

12. Neetu wants to purchase a doll for ₹ 40. Which of the following set of money can she use to purchase the doll?

(a)

(b)

(c)

(d)

13. Raghav has ₹ 50 . He pays ₹ 20 for 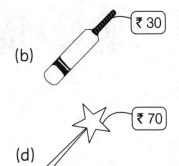 . Now, he can

purchase _____ .

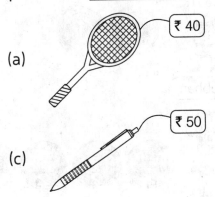

(a) ₹ 40

(b) ₹ 30

(c) ₹ 50

(d) ₹ 70

14. Which one of the following set of money is more than hundred rupee?

(a)

(b)

(c)

(d)

15. Rahul has ₹ 90. Which one of the following can he buy?

(a) A doll ₹ 100

(b) A toy car ₹ 120

(c) A toy ₹ 75

(d) A pencil box for ₹ 95

16. Which boy saved the less amount?

17. Match the item with the set of money needed to purchase it.

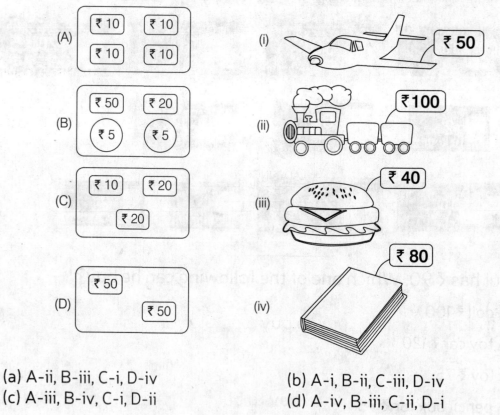

(a) A-ii, B-iii, C-i, D-iv
(c) A-iii, B-iv, C-i, D-ii

(b) A-i, B-ii, C-iii, D-iv
(d) A-iv, B-iii, C-ii, D-i

Observe the price tags and answer the questions (18-20).

LUNCH BOX	BOTTLE	SOCKS	BOOK
₹ 40	₹ 25	₹ 50	₹ 80

18. Seema has ₹ 50. How much more money does she need to buy the book?

(a) ₹ 10   (b) ₹ 30   (c) ₹ 20   (d) No need

19. Which item has the lowest amount?

(a) Lunch Box   (b) Bottle   (c) Socks   (d) Book

20. Akshay bought a lunch box and a bottle for himself. The bill paid by him was _____.

(a) ₹ 90   (b) ₹ 65   (c) ₹ 85   (d) ₹ 50

Look at the price of each vegetables and answer the questions (21-23).

POTATO	TOMATO	LADYFINGER	CARROT	BRINJAL
₹ 5	₹ 4	₹ 3	₹ 2	₹ 6

21. Three carrots will cost ₹ _____.

(a) 2   (b) 4   (c) 6   (d) 8

22. How much money do I pay to buy a potato?

(a) ₹ 5   (b) ₹ 4   (c) ₹ 6   (d) ₹ 3

23. How much more money do I pay to buy a brinjal than a tomato?

(a) ₹ 3   (b) ₹ 2   (c) ₹ 4   (d) ₹ 1

8

Shapes and Patterns

1. Which shape is a cylinder?

  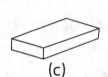

   (a)   (b)   (c)   (d)

2. Which shape is a sphere?

   (a)   (b)   (c)   (d)

3. What is the shape of a softy ?

   (a) Cuboid   (b) Cone   (c) Rectangle   (d) Square

4. Which shape is not shown in the box?

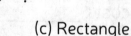

   (a) Rectangle   (b) Cuboid   (c) Cone   (d) Cylinder

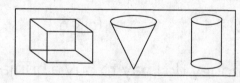

5. Match the following with their correct names and shapes.

	Column I			Column II
(A)	◯	(i)		Cone
(B)	△	(ii)		Cylinder
(C)	▭	(iii)		Cuboid
(D)	cuboid	(iv)		Circle
(E)	cone	(v)		Rectangle
(F)	cylinder	(vi)		Triangle

	(A)	(B)	(C)	(D)	(E)	(F)
(a)	(iii)	(iv)	(iii)	(i)	(v)	(vi)
(b)	(v)	(vi)	(iv)	(iii)	(iv)	(i)
(c)	(iv)	(vi)	(v)	(iii)	(i)	(ii)
(d)	(vi)	(i)	(ii)	(v)	(iv)	(iii)

6. Name the shape of an objects kept on the table.

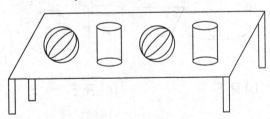

(a) Triangle and Cylinder   (b) Cylinder and Sphere

(c) Circle and Cone   (d) Sphere and Rectangle

7. Pepsi cane  is in _____ shape.

(a) cylinder   (b) sphere   (c) rectangle   (d) circle

8. Choose the odd one out.

(a)

(b)

(c)

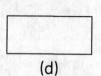
(d)

9. The shape of the shaded region is a _____.

(a) triangle   (b) rectangle   (c) circle   (d) square

10. Which of the following is matched correctly?

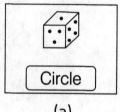
(a)

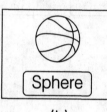
(b)

(c)

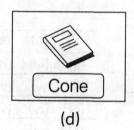
(d)

11. Shapes _____ and _____ will combine to form a cone.

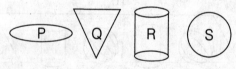

(a) P, Q   (b) P, S   (c) R, S   (d) R, P

12. Complete the following pattern.

    ___

(a)   (b) □   (c) △   (d) None of these

13. What will be the next figure to complete the pattern?

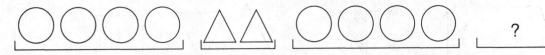

(a) ◯◯◯

(b) △△△△

(c) ◯◯◯◯

(d) △△

14. What comes next in the given pattern?

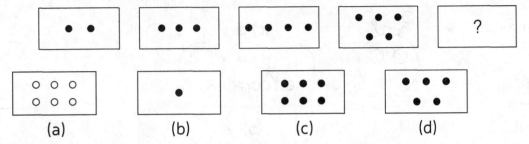

(a)   (b)   (c)   (d)

15. Complete the following pattern.

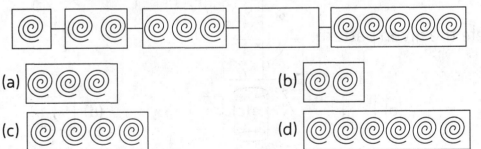

(a)   (b)

(c)   (d)

16. What comes next in the given pattern?

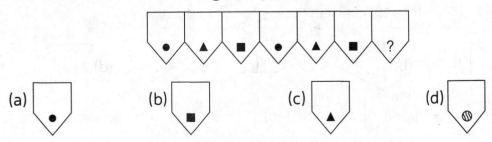

(a)   (b)   (c)   (d)

17. Choose the correct option that completes the pattern given below.

(a)   (b)   (c)   (d)

18. Total number of circles in the given figure is _____ .

(a) 11   (b) 12

(c) 13   (d) 10

19. Complete the given pattern.

(a)   (b)   (c)   (d)

20. Which shape will be best to complete the given triangle?

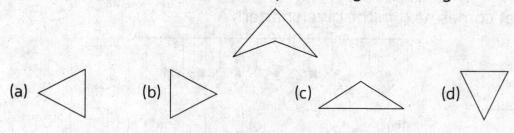

(a)   (b)   (c)   (d)

21. Which piece can be put together to make a complete rectangle?

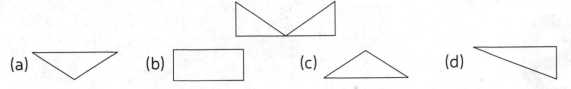

(a) (b) (c) (d)

22. Look at the following pattern.

How would you show this pattern using letters?

(a) ABC (b) ABA (c) ABB (d) None of these

23. Look at the following pattern.

How would you show this pattern using letters?

(a) ABAB (b) AABB (c) ABBB (d) ABBA

24. Study the following pattern and choose correct answer.

50, 55, 60, 65, 70, 75, ...

(a) Skip counting by 5 (b) Skip counting by 2

(c) Skip counting by 3 (d) Skip counting by 4

25. Total number of sides in the given star is _____ .

(a) 9 (b) 10 (c) 5 (d) 11

9

Picture Graphs

Look at the picture graphs of different toys given below and answer the questions (1-6).

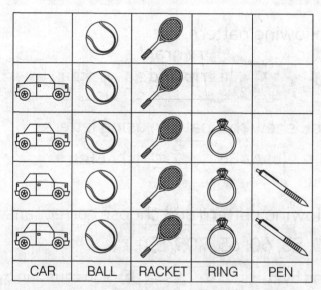

1. Which toy is least in number?

   (a) Car   (b) Pen   (c) Ball   (d) Ring

2. Which two toys are same in numbers?

   (a) Cars and Balls   (b) Balls and Rings

   (c) Balls and Rackets   (d) Rings and Pens

3. How many are there?

(a) 3   (b) 4   (c) 5   (d) 6

4. How many 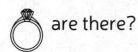 are there?

(a) 4   (b) 5   (c) 6   (d) 7

5. How many more rackets are there than rings?

(a) 5   (b) 2   (c) 3   (d) 0

6. How many less cars are there than balls?

(a) 1   (b) 0   (c) 2   (d) 3

Look at the following picture graphs, which shows the number of animals seen by Ram in a trip and answer the questions (7-11).

7. How many monkeys were seen by Ram?

(a) 4   (b) 3   (c) 2   (d) 5

8. There were _____ more cows than cats.

(a) 1   (b) 2   (c) 3   (d) 4

9. There were _____ animals altogether.

    (a) 11   (b) 13   (c) 16   (d) 14

10. Which two animals are equal in numbers?

    (a) Cats and Horses   (b) Cows and Cats

    (c) Dogs and Monkeys   (d) Cows and Monkeys

11. Which animal is greater than dogs but lesser than monkeys?

    (a) Cow   (b) Horse   (c) Cat   (d) Dog

The graph given below shows the number of pencils sold in a week. Study the graph and answer the questions (12-15).

12. How many pencils were sold on Thursday?

    (a) 2   (b) 4   (c) 3   (d) 5

13. On which day, the minimum number of pencils were sold?

    (a) Monday   (b) Tuesday   (c) Wednesday   (d) Thursday

14. On which day, two pencils were sold?

    (a) Monday   (b) Tuesday   (c) Friday   (d) Wednesday

15. What is the total number of pencils sold from Monday to Wednesday?

    (a) 5   (b) 6   (c) 7   (d) 8

The quantities of different vegetables grown by a farmer into his garden is shown below and now, answer the questions (16-18).

Vegetables names	Number of vegetables
Carrots	🥕🥕🥕🥕🥕🥕🥕🥕
Potatoes	🥔🥔🥔🥔🥔
Mushrooms	🍄🍄🍄🍄🍄🍄
Brinjals	🍆🍆🍆🍆

16. Difference between the number of carrots and mushrooms is _____ .

    (a) 1   (b) 2   (c) 3   (d) 4

17. How many potatoes are grown into the garden?

    (a) 4   (b) 5   (c) 6   (d) 8

18. _____ types of vegetables are grown by the farmer into his garden.

    (a) 5   (b) 6   (c) 4   (d) 3

Look at the picture given below to answer the given question.

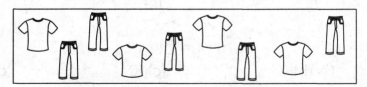

19. Which table shows the correct number of T-shirts and Pants?

(a)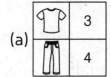
(b)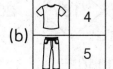
(c)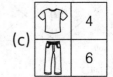
(d)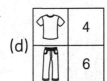

Practice Set 1

A Test Based on the Whole Content

1. What shape is missing in the given pattern?

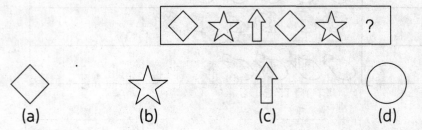

(a) (b) (c) (d)

2. How many more ☆ do you need to balance the scale, if 1☆ = 1○?

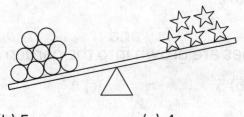

(a) 3　　　(b) 5　　　(c) 4　　　(d) 6

3. Number of circles in the given figure are _____.

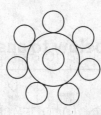

(a) 8　　　(b) 9　　　(c) 10　　　(d) 10

4. Fill the missing number in the given pattern.

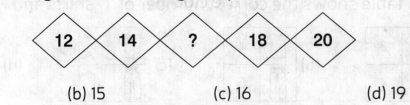

(a) 10　　　(b) 15　　　(c) 16　　　(d) 19

5. Complete the given pattern.

3 A , 5 B , 7 C , 9 D , ☐ , 13 F

(a) 11 H   (b) 10 E   (c) 11 D   (d) 11 E

6. My mother has 12 potatoes. She uses 6 potatoes. How many potatoes are left with her?

(a) 5   (b) 7   (c) 6   (d) 8

7. Fill the appropriate number in the box.

| 2 tens | 3 ones | + | 5 tens | 1 one | = | ? | 4 ones |

(a) 6 tens   (b) 8 tens   (c) 7 tens   (d) 9 tens

8. If the last month was January and the next month is March. Which month is now?

(a) May   (b) April   (c) June   (d) February

9. Which day comes before Sunday?

(a) Monday   (b) Tuesday   (c) Saturday   (d) Wednesday

10. If an ice-cream costs ₹ 10 and a chocolate costs ₹ 5. How much total money Rahul needs to buy one ice-cream and two chocolates?

(a) ₹ 15   (b) ₹ 20   (c) ₹ 28   (d) ₹ 10

11. What is the time shown in the clock?

(a) 2 O'clock   (b) 4 O'clock

(c) 3 O'clock   (d) 5 O'clock

12. How many eight are there in the given sum?

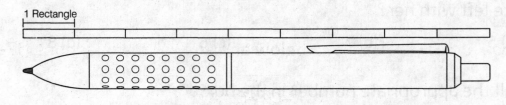

$$43 \quad + \quad 45 \quad = \quad ?$$

(a) 2   (b) 4   (c) 3   (d) 1

13. How many rectangles long is the pen?

1 Rectangle

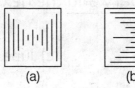

(a) 9   (b) 8

(c) 10   (d) 7

14. Which box has more lines?

(a)   (b)

(a) A   (b) B

(c) Both have equal lines   (d) None of these

15. Which of the following two shapes make a total weight of 10 kg?

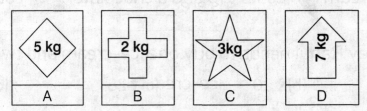

5 kg	2 kg	3kg	7 kg
A	B	C	D

(a) A and D   (b) B and C

(c) C and D   (d) B and D

16. Weight of the box is _____.

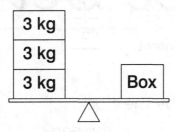

(a) 8 kg   (b) 10 kg   (c) 9 kg   (d) 11 kg

Look at the picture given below and answer the questions (17-20).

Toffee	
Ice-cream	
Balloon	
Car	

17. How many more toffees are there than ice-creams?

(a) 1   (b) 3   (c) 2   (d) 4

18. Which item is four in number?

(a) Car   (b) Ice-cream   (c) Balloon   (d) Toffee

19. Total number of all the items are _____.

(a) 12   (b) 11   (c) 14   (d) 13

20. I am more in numbers than ice-creams but less in numbers than toffees. What I am?

(a) Car   (b) Balloon   (c) Ice-cream   (d) Toffee

Practice Set 2

A Test Based on the Whole Content

1. Mark the time shown by the clock.

   (a) 11 O'clock   (b) 12 O'clock   (c) 10 O'clock   (d) 4 O'clock

2. Raghav has 6 toy cars. He gave 2 toy cars to his sister. How many toy cars are left with him?

   (a) 3   (b) 5   (c) 4   (d) 6

3. Choose the option having numbers arranged in ascending order.

   (a) 24, 36, 15, 20, 11   (b) 15, 16, 20, 19, 35

   (c) 11, 14, 22, 35, 46   (d) 45, 11, 15, 6, 17

4. Starting with Monday, which is the fourth day of the week?

   (a) Wednesday   (b) Thursday

   (c) Tuesday   (d) Friday

5. Fill the box with correct number.

   | 7 tens 4 ones | – | 4 tens 2 ones | = | 3 tens ? ones |

   (a) 1   (b) 3   (c) 2   (d) 4

6. Add the money and choose the correct option.

 + 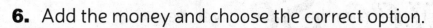 + = ?

(a) ₹ 25   (b) ₹ 15   (c) ₹ 20   (d) ₹ 5

7. Fill the missing numbers counting by 2.

44	46	?	50	52	?	?

(a) 47, 53, 54   (b) 48, 54, 56   (c) 47, 54, 56   (d) 48, 50, 54

8. Which one of the following numbers is more than $6 + 5$?

(a) 12   (b) 8   (c) 9   (d) 10

9. How many squares are there in the given figure?

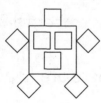

(a) 9   (b) 8   (c) 7   (d) 10

10. Which one of the following coin has the highest value?

(a)   (b)   (c)   (d)

11. Which of the following is in triangular shape?

(a)   (b)   (c)   (d)

12. Choose the correct sum from the abacus given below.

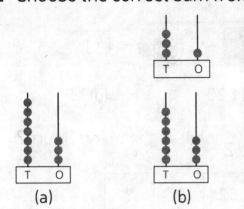 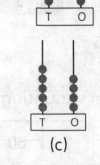 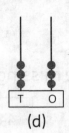

| (a) | (b) | (c) | (d) |

13. If Sunday is the first day of the week, then name the last day of the week?

(a) Monday (b) Tuesday (c) Wednesday (d) Saturday

14. Smith is reading a book. He is on page number 20. The next page number will be _____.

(a) 23 (b) 19 (c) 21 (d) 22

15. In a class of 28 children, there are 12 boys. How many girls are there in the class?

(a) 14 (b) 15 (c) 16 (d) 17

16. Match the following.

	Column I		Column II
A.	17 − 15	(i)	15
B.	9 + 4	(ii)	2
C.	15 − 0	(iii)	11
D.	8 + 3	(iv)	13

	A	B	C	D
(a)	(ii)	(iv)	(i)	(iii)
(b)	(i)	(ii)	(iii)	(iv)
(c)	(i)	(iv)	(i)	(ii)
(d)	(i)	(ii)	(iii)	(i)

17. Which of the following shapes in not present in the given figure?

(a) Cylinder   (b) Circle   (c) Rectangle   (d) Triangle

18. Which of the following option shows the least value?

(a)    (b)   (c)   (d)

19. Complete the pattern given below.

$ $ ★ ★ ★ $ $ ★ ★ ★ ⬚?⬚

(a) ★ ★   (b) ★ $ (c) $ $ (d) $ ★

20. Joy has ₹ 70 , then which one of the following can he buy?

   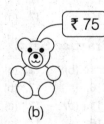   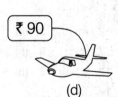

₹ 80   ₹ 75   ₹ 70   ₹ 90

(a)   (b)   (c)   (d)

Answers

Chapter 1 : Play with Numbers

1. (d)	**2.** (b)	**3.** (b)	**4.** (b)	**5.** (a)
6. (a)	**7.** (a)	**8.** (a)	**9.** (c)	**10.** (b)
11. (a)	**12.** (c)	**13.** (d)	**14.** (c)	**15.** (a)
16. (b)	**17.** (d)	**18.** (b)	**19.** (a)	**20.** (b)
21. (c)	**22.** (b)	**23.** (a)	**24.** (a)	**25.** (b)
26. (c)	**27.** (a)	**28.** (b)	**29.** (b)	**30.** (c)

Chapter 2 : Addition

1. (b)	**2.** (a)	**3.** (b)	**4.** (b)	**5.** (b)
6. (b)	**7.** (b)	**8.** (b)	**9.** (a)	**10.** (b)
11. (b)	**12.** (b)	**13.** (b)	**14.** (a)	**15.** (b)
16. (d)	**17.** (b)	**18.** (c)	**19.** (b)	**20.** (a)
21. (b)	**22.** (c)	**23.** (c)	**24.** (a)	**25.** (c)
26. (c)	**27.** (c)	**28.** (c)	**29.** (a)	

Chapter 3 : Subtraction

1. (b)	**2.** (b)	**3.** (b)	**4.** (b)	**5.** (c)
6. (a)	**7.** (a)	**8.** (c)	**9.** (a)	**10.** (a)
11. (a)	**12.** (a)	**13.** (b)	**14.** (c)	**15.** (c)
16. (c)	**17.** (a)	**18.** (c)	**19.** (a)	**20.** (b)
21. (a)	**22.** (d)	**23.** (c)	**24.** (c)	**25.** (a)
26. (c)	**27.** (c)			

Chapter 4 : Length

1. (b)	**2.** (d)	**3.** (c)	**4.** (d)	**5.** (d)
6. (c)	**7.** (c)	**8.** (a)	**9.** (b)	**10.** (a)
11. (b)	**12.** (d)	**13.** (b)	**14.** (b)	**15.** (b)
16. (a)	**17.** (b)			

Chapter 5 : Weight

1. (b)	**2.** (b)	**3.** (c)	**4.** (b)	**5.** (c)
6. (c)	**7.** (b)	**8.** (b)	**9.** (b)	**10.** (b)
11. (b)	**12.** (c)	**13.** (b)	**14.** (c)	**15.** (b)
16. (a)	**17.** (c)			

Chapter 6 : Time and Calendar

1. (b)	**2.** (b)	**3.** (b)	**4.** (d)	**5.** (b)
6. (a)	**7.** (b)	**8.** (b)	**9.** (c)	**10.** (b)
11. (b)	**12.** (d)	**13.** (b)	**14.** (c)	**15.** (a)
16. (d)	**17.** (c)	**18.** (b)	**19.** [i] (c)	[ii] (a)
20. (a)	**21.** (b)	**22.** (c)	**23.** (b)	**24.** (a)
25. (a)	**26.** (b)	**27.** (c)	**28.** (b)	

Chapter 7 : Money

1. (b)	**2.** (c)	**3.** (b)	**4.** (b)	**5.** (b)
6. (c)	**7.** (b)	**8.** (c)	**9.** (a)	**10.** (c)
11. (a)	**12.** (a)	**13.** (b)	**14.** (b)	**15.** (c)
16. (b)	**17.** (c)	**18.** (b)	**19.** (b)	**20.** (b)
21. (c)	**22.** (a)	**23.** (b)		

Chapter 8 : Shapes and Patterns

1. (b)	**2.** (b)	**3.** (b)	**4.** (a)	**5.** (c)
6. (b)	**7.** (a)	**8.** (c)	**9.** (d)	**10.** (b)
11. (a)	**12.** (c)	**13.** (d)	**14.** (c)	**15.** (c)
16. (a)	**17.** (b)	**18.** (a)	**19.** (c)	**20.** (c)
21. (a)	**22.** (c)	**23.** (c)	**24.** (a)	**25.** (b)

Chapter 9 : Picture Graphs

1. (b)	**2.** (c)	**3.** (a)	**4.** (c)	**5.** (b)
6. (a)	**7.** (d)	**8.** (b)	**9.** (c)	**10.** (a)
11. (a)	**12.** (b)	**13.** (a)	**14.** (d)	**15.** (b)
16. (b)	**17.** (b)	**18.** (c)	**19.** (b)	

Practice Set 1

1. (c)	**2.** (c)	**3.** (b)	**4.** (c)	**5.** (d)
6. (c)	**7.** (c)	**8.** (d)	**9.** (c)	**10.** (b)
11. (c)	**12.** (a)	**13.** (a)	**14.** (c)	**15.** (c)
16. (c)	**17.** (c)	**18.** (c)	**19.** (d)	**20.** (b)

Practice Set 2

1. (b)	**2.** (c)	**3.** (c)	**4.** (b)	**5.** (c)
6. (a)	**7.** (b)	**8.** (a)	**9.** (a)	**10.** (c)
11. (b)	**12.** (a)	**13.** (d)	**14.** (c)	**15.** (c)
16. (a)	**17.** (a)	**18.** (d)	**19.** (c)	**20.** (c)